How to Grow
Club Membership
Using the Internet

By Al Kernek

Practical Online Strategies for Non-Techies

Table of Contents

Chapter 3: How to Get Your Club Website to Appear on the First Page of Search Engine Results! 15

Introduction

You belong to a club or are interested in starting a club. Your club may be small or large. It could be a garden club, a club for playing cards, one to share coin or stamp collections, a local stock market investment club, a Toastmasters club to help people improve their public speaking skills, or even a local chapter of the Elks or Rotary Club. Regardless of the size or purpose, the common ingredient for success for any club is recruiting and maintaining a healthy membership.

Club membership is always in flux. For a variety of reasons, members come and go. Some move away; some find themselves faced with new obligations that interfere with continued membership. Without a steady stream of new dues-paying members coming in, the vitality and operating budget of any club can dry up.

You probably already recognize that the lifeblood of any club is an affordable process for recruiting new members. Like an aching tooth, it is a situation that just won't go away. The eternal dilemma faced by most social clubs is how to recruit new membership within the financial constraints of a limited budget.

Perhaps you have tried traditional methods like local press releases, word of mouth and flyers, but they yield sporadic or little results.

And more visible community outreaches, like newspaper and magazine advertising, are expensive. Most likely, however, your club doesn't have a large budget.

So you ask yourself, "Is there a way to generate a steady flow of new members without spending a lot of money?" The answer is a resounding, "Yes!"

What this Book will tell You

You will learn how to implement a proven strategy for using the Internet to inexpensively grow your club membership. Whether your club is just starting out, is a local club, or a national or worldwide entity, you will discover how to use online tools to boost membership with very little out-of-pocket expense. This works!

The easy-to-understand action plans presented within these pages have actually been used to double the membership of a club within ten months. The plans satisfy several important goals:

- Must be achievable within a club budget focused on local membership. Most small clubs have an income that is determined by dues and perhaps events (raffles, cookie sales, etc.). Money is tight and must be allocated judiciously.

- Cumulative revenues emanating from additional dues paid by new members should cover the cost of the Internet marketing strategies outlined in this book. In other words, the recruitment process should pay for itself!

- The steps outlined herein must be capable of implementation by any typical PC user, rather than requiring the services of a technical guru.

- The strategy must be scalable, so that it works for both large and small clubs.

You are about to benefit from extensive research and years of Internet marketing experience. The information conveyed within these pages will show you how to best implement online marketing for your club while avoiding costly pitfalls and considerable frustration. By following the guidelines outlined herein, your club will achieve superior results and likely save hundreds of dollars.

Why I Know It Works

I am an Internet marketing consultant who does this for a living. So it was natural for me to volunteer my experience and expertise to help my Toastmaster club (www.rbtoastmasters.com) increase its membership. Following much research and some experimentation, I came up with the unique set of online tactics that I am going to share with you in these pages.

Suffice it to say that the results speak for themselves:

- My Toastmaster club achieved a highly visible Website, one designed to attract likely members from the local area. This site also serves as an administrative center for the club, making it easy to distribute timely information to members.

- Club membership almost doubled within a ten-month period and is still growing at an average rate of two new members monthly.

- The total Internet marketing expenses for this period were about $250. Dues collected from new members totaled $630. The project has more than paid for itself.

Assumptions about You, the Reader

It is assumed that you have not been living in a cave for the past ten years, cut off from civilization. That is, you are familiar with the Internet and Websites. "Surfing" the Internet by using search engines (such as Google or Yahoo) to find information, products or services is something you have done many times. You have navigated through Websites, and you generally understand their nature and how they are typically presented.

That's it! If you are a typical PC user who is familiar with applications like Microsoft Word, then the information presented in these pages is easily grasped. I have minimized technical jargon and focused on explaining just what you need to know. Subjects that you do not need to be concerned about are purposely excluded, and additional resources are abundantly presented.

There's just one catch. You have to be willing to invest your time in doing the work to create and maintain online promotional vehicles! Fortunately, this is an easy task today and one that will not consume an inordinate amount of time. So you might as well invest a little time and learn how to promote your club yourself.

This book is truly a proven roadmap that will lead to a successful process for growing your club membership. Enjoy the journey.

Chapter 1: Setting Up Your Club Website

It is difficult to grow club membership without a Website. Your Website is a virtual clubhouse that "sells" site visitors on the merits of joining you club.

No business today would think about not having a Website. It is a critical aspect of marketing goods and services. Over ninety percent of the world now turns to the Internet for shopping and information. Without a club Website, your organization is "invisible" to prospective members who are hunting for a club just like yours to join.

An Online Marketing Vehicle for Attracting New Members

If you approach your club as a business whose success is measured in terms of a growing membership, the advantages of having a club Website become readily apparent:

- It opens up a worldwide market for your club, or conversely can be focused to target a local market.

- Websites are available to the public 24 hours daily, 7 days per week on a year-round basis.

- It gives you the same marketing clout as much larger clubs.

- The possibility of offering salable goods and services, such as t-shirts or coffee cups, exist through ecommerce. If you wish, the site can be automated to take and process orders while you sleep.

- Your club can also collect dues by allowing members to make secure online payments using their credit cards.

- Online forms can capture "sales leads" from prospective members.

- An attractive, informative site enhances club credibility.

- A club Website provides a means of making information available to members, prospective members and the public.

- Your club Website simplifies member support by offering online information, such as answers to frequently asked questions, easy access to club rules or meeting schedules, and a simple means of communicating with club leadership.

Launching a Club Website is Readily Affordable

When it comes to Websites, the first question usually asked by club leaders is "Can we afford our own Website?" The answer is unequivocally, "Yes!"

The Internet has become so pervasive and mature that hosting a Website now costs just pennies a day. And there are a ton of Internet Service Providers hungry for your business.

A Quick Website Primer

There are two basic elements that form the foundation of any Website:

- ISP: Websites physically exist on a server that is located somewhere (you don't care where!) and connected to the World Wide Web (i.e., the "Internet") via high-speed communications lines. Your club Website will be "hosted" (i.e., reside) on such a server. This service is provided by a commercial Internet Service Provider (ISP).

- URL: The way people find your Website is through a unique address – your Uniform Resource Locator (URL), more commonly known as a "domain name" or "Website address." Think of a huge telephone book containing all of the Web addresses in the world. "Dialing" the URL connects you to the requested Website.

So, when someone types your unique Website address (e.g., www.myclub.com) into a Web browser, this identifies and retrieves your Website. It's that simple.

How Much does it Cost to Launch a Website?

Not much. Internet Service Providers offer subscription fees for both Website hosting and domain name registration. Typically, both cost less than $70 annually.

Choosing a Good ISP is Important!

Since your club is going to be "married" to its ISP for a long time, selecting a good hosting provider is important. Once you launch a Website with a particular ISP, switching to another ISP is technically complex.

What You Should Seek in an ISP

The major qualities to seek are:

- Sufficient size and company longevity so that you can have confidence they will be around even in a down economy.

- The ability to research domain names by them trying out to determine which ones are taken and which are available for registration.

- Inexpensive Web hosting that provides adequate disk space, high performance, security and automatic backups.

- An abundance of tools to support your Website development, such as templates, preparation tools, file upload capabilities, tutorials, FAQs, and access to support personnel.

- Free email addresses along with Website hosting. For example, if your domain name is www.mycarclub.com, then your club should be able to set up free email addresses such as "president@mycarclub.com."

Recommended ISP

Fortunately, you do not have to go through the time-consuming and often difficult task of identifying good ISPs which satisfy the above criteria. I have done that for you.

As a professional Internet marketing consultant, I have worked with many ISPs. Of all of them – and each has strengths - I am most comfortable with www.GoDaddy.com. They provide the functionality and resources to meet the needs of most clubs:

- There are no set-up fees. Annual fees start under $60 for a robust, high-performance Website hosting solution.

- Domain name research tools are available to help you quickly resolve on a Website address to suit your needs, one with an annual registration fee of $10-$15.

- A structured process leads you through everything necessary to set up a domain name and the best hosting package for your needs (which for most clubs is the Economy Plan).

- Up to 100 free email addresses are included with Website hosting.

- A complete "Website Tonight" option is available that includes hosting, email, etc., along with access to a function-rich package for building your own Website. Website Tonight includes over 90 pre-built, customizable Website templates to choose from. Three plans offer economical pricing based on the number of pages your Website will have, ranging from five dollars to thirteen dollars monthly. This is a good option for those who do not have Web development experience or PC-based software to prepare a Website.

- GoDaddy is a major ISP that is not going away, even if the economy tanks.

- They guarantee 99.9 percent uptime for your Website server, and provide free backups to ensure nothing is lost if disaster strikes.

- Provide good, online tutorials and FAQs.

- Offers 24/7 free technical support. GoDaddy has knowledgeable, responsive personnel that are only a phone call away. Optional ongoing support plans for maintenance and updates are also available.

Of course, you can easily shop for other ISP offerings. Two sites – www.hostcritique.net and www.top-10-web-hosting.com provide an easy means to accomplish this.

Things to Avoid

Here are some "gotchas" to avoid as you consider which ISP to choose as a host for your club Website:

- Avoid hosting solutions that are advertised as "free." They typically place advertising on your site, which can be discontinued only if you pay as much as you would to have your own independent hosting solution. Moreover, any work and expense you perform to promote your "free" site actually benefits the parent hosting company rather than investing in your club's long-term Internet visibility.

- Stay away from Yahoo Website hosting solutions. They offer easy-to-use development tools, but these contain unique functionality that makes it difficult to transfer your site to another ISP down the road if you are unsatisfied with Yahoo's services.

- Watch out for ISPs that offer "starter" rates for the first year which thereafter could increase substantially.

What's in a Domain Name?

One of the most important decisions in launching a club Website is the selection of a domain name (i.e., your Website address). Obviously, it should reflect the name of your club, but including keyword terms is important as well.

Keywords are terms or phrases that someone is likely to enter into a search engine box when hunting for a specific type of club in a certain geographical location. Having your major keywords in the domain name boosts the chances of your site showing up within the search engine results.

For example, suppose *www.FallbrookRifleClub.com* is chosen as the domain name for the Veterans Rifle Club located in the town of Fallbrook. This is good domain name choice, since it contains the keywords "Fallbrook" and "Rifle".

In our example, someone searching for a rifle club in the town of Fallbrook who enters "Fallbrook rifle club" in Google is likely to see www.fallbrookrifleclub.com at the top of the search engine results.

Another domain name choice could have been *www.FallbrookVeteransRifleClub.com*, which would likely yield similar search engine returns plus add those who are seeking a local rifle club whose members are veterans.

Ideally, a domain name should be easy to remember, something you can tell people that is easily recallable. Generally speaking, the shorter a domain name the better, and try to avoid the use of hyphens or underscores.

Thus it pays to give some thought to what keywords identify your club before choosing a domain name.

.COM or .ORG?

Domain names for non-profit organizations usually have a ".org" extension, such as *www.SmallTownCoinClub.org* or *www.ChildrensHelp.org*. However, the ".com" extension is more common in the Internet world, and many people will automatically type it into a browser without thinking. If your domain name ends in a ".org," you may lose a site visitor. The choice is yours.

There are more types of extensions. Because the Internet is growing astronomically, other extensions have been added (like new area codes for phone numbers) to allow more Websites to have meaningful domain names. These include ".net" and ".biz." My advice is to stay away from anything but a ".org" or ".com" extension for a club Website, as most people are unfamiliar with the others and may not be able to find your site if they manually type your domain name into an Internet browser with the wrong extension.

Register Alternative Domain Names?

Most ISPs will present alternative domain names with extensions other than ".org" or ".com," and urge you to register those as well, playing on the fear than someone else will steal your thunder by doing so. For a club site, I think this is unnecessary and a wasteful expense.

However, it often pays to register the same domain name under ".org" or ".com" extensions if you have local competition for the activities on which your club is focused.

Another consideration is to think of several keyword-laden domain names and register the best of them. This keeps strong permutations out of competitive hands. It also presents the opportunity to set it up so that these extra domain names also "point" to your club Website.

For example, when someone enters fallbrookveteransrifleclub.com into a browser, that domain can be set to automatically bring up the Website whose address is www.fallbrookrifleclub.com. Doing this gives your club more keyword-packed domains for search engines as well.

Chapter 2: Your Website Content

Once you have selected a hosting vendor and registered one or more domain names for your club Website, it is time to create the actual site itself.

The best way to do this is to plan everything out in advance before a single page is created. Remember, everything on your club site has to work together in an intuitive fashion. You will save time and avoid frustration by sketching out the Website flow and basic navigation system beforehand.

Capture Prospective Club Members with a Friendly Website

In creating your club Website, it is crucial to bear in mind your target audience. What is the profile of typical club members – their background, likes and dislikes? Prepare your Website content for them, and you are likely to enjoy more success in attracting new members.

Ensure You Implement Good Website Structure

There are also some essential basics that bear reminding:

- Have a Website banner graphic with a meaningful tagline (i.e., a catchy phrase that brands your site).

- Clicking on the banner should always take a visitor back to the Home page.

- Employ the same navigation links at the same position on each Webpage. Many "self developed" club sites often have dead-end pages without any means of going somewhere else other than clicking on a browser's "back" button. Every Webpage should afford easy access to all other Webpages.

- At minimum, include Webpages for Home, About Us, Schedule or Activities, Location/Time/Facilities, and Contact Us.

Make Visitors Feel Comfortable in Selecting your Club

An important aspect of a club Website is to make visitors comfortable with your club and its members.

To accomplish this, make sure your club purpose is fully explained in simple-to-understand language. Appeal to prospective new members by writing benefits-oriented copy and using graphics wherever appropriate to enhance visual attractiveness.

Sprinkle testimonials from club members around the site. This enhances credibility and helps prospective members feel comfortable in paying the club a visit.

Include Member Photos

Most prospective new members have one thing in common – they are nervous about fitting into a club. Is this the right group of people for me? Are they in my age group? Will they like me, and will I like them?

Surveys have shown that including photographs of club members and activities plays a significant role in enticing possible members to take that crucial next step and contact the club to attend a meeting.

Add a Link to GoogleMap or MapQuest

If someone is interested enough to seek directions to your club's meeting facility, don't risk losing them by making it hard to find. Many clubs have a static map on their Location page. But it is best to include a link to GoogleMap or MapQuest that allows the site visitor to obtain custom direction from their home or office to the club's facility.

Offer Multiple Means of Contacting the Club

Make taking that first step to contacting the club easy by providing three methods – a phone number, email address and a contact form. This way, prospective members can chose the method that best suits their inclination, and your club will receive more inquiries.

Your Website is for Members Too

Ideally, your club Website will be designed for club members too. It should be a place where members can access the latest information no matter where they happen to be.

Add useful Member Information

Club schedules, activities and duties can easily be disseminated on a central Website. This saves a lot of time for club leadership, since everything can be posted in a single, online location just once.

And setting up a list of club email addresses (e.g., treasurer@myclub.com) on the site allows members to communicate with club officers without having to know the personal addresses to which these emails are forwarded. It is easy to change email forwarding addresses whenever new officers are elected.

Finally, downloadable materials can be placed on a club Website for members. These can include duty manuals, forms, notices, and certificates…basically anything a club desires. Microsoft Word documents should first be converted to non-modifiable PDF format. Place an icon linked to the free Adobe PDF reader on pages where downloadable materials are offered.

Collect Dues through Online Debit and Credit Card Payments

One way to make dues collection easier for the club treasurer and members alike is to offer the option of paying online using any major credit card.

With a free PayPal account (www.paypal.com), this is easy to do:

- Low transaction fees: 1.9% to 2.9% + $0.30 USD

- No monthly, set-up, or cancellation fees

- Get paid by anyone, even by customers without a PayPal account

- Accept credit cards, debit cards, bank transfers, and PayPal

It is best to set up a separate page for online dues payment. The dues amount and payment schedule can be explained there, along any special instructions.

 PayPal has an excellent, easy to understand process that leads you through the creation of a coded button to place on your club Website. This requires insertion of some HTML code into your payment Webpage. However, GoDaddy tools and HTML editors offered by most ISPs make this easy to accomplish.

Once your "Buy Now" or "Subscribe" button is in-place on the "Dues Payment" page of your club Website, clicking on it transparently transfers the user to a form on the PayPal Website where a credit or debit card transaction is completed.

Two points to remember are:

- Be sure to add the PayPal fee to the online dues payment amount so that after the transaction is completed, the club will receive the correct sum. For example, if monthly dues are $20, then any member who pays online should be instructed to pay $20.88 to cover the PayPal 2.9 percent transaction fee and $.30 fixed fee. You can set this amount up during the PayPal button creation process.

- Go through the PayPal process to set up electronic transfers so you can transfer collected dues to your club bank account upon request.

Chapter 3: How to Get Your Club Website to Appear on the First Page of Search Engine Results!

When someone uses Google, Yahoo or MSN to search for functions and activities offered by your club, the goal is to have your club Website appear on the first page of the organic search engine returns. Studies have demonstrated that search engine users rarely look beyond the first three pages. If your site does not show up within the first three pages of results, it remains "invisible" on the Internet for all practical purposes.

Achieving a first page result for a search engine return is "golden" for your club. It immediately conveys credibility to your club site. Think of it as having been "blessed" by the search engine as being one of the best answers for what the user is seeking. It is like free advertising. And, your club Website will receive significantly more traffic once it attains first page ranking by major search engines.

Each search engine employs unique algorithms to determine how to rank their returns. One is their assessment of how relevant your site is to the words or phrases entered by the user into the search box. Then, the returned sites are ranked according to each search engine's determination of popularity.

Optimizing a Website for the major search engines is both an art and a science. It requires both technical skill and experience. I am not going to attempt to teach you the full range of search engine optimization techniques. Rather, you will learn here exactly what steps to take to enhance the chances that your club Website eventually shows up on the first page of returns for any major search engine.

The key is to understand how search engines think and how they go about indexing your site. Search engines want your site to succeed. If you follow the steps outlined in this Chapter, your site will ultimately appear within the first three pages of a search engine results...and hopefully in the first position on the first page.

Step 1 - Determine your Keywords

For your purposes, "keywords" are those words or phrases that you would expect a prospective member to type into a search engine when seeking the activities offered by your club.

A prospective club member may not know about your club. Hence, in addition to your club name you need to identify generic keywords that best describe your club's main purpose and benefits.

For example, if someone wants to improve their public speaking and communication skills, they would likely type "public speaking presentation skills" into a search engine box.

Their first result would yield solutions from around the world. But this person lives in Anytown, USA, and he/she wants a local answer. So they refine their search by typing "public speaking communication skills anytown" into the search engine box. Now, the returns that offer a solution within "Anytown" are displayed first as the most relevant answer.

Your Club Name is Always a Keyword

As your club grows, people will become aware of its existence. Some may perform searches based on the club name. Hence, your club name should always be one of your primary keywords. This is especially true for local clubs that are chapters of a larger national or worldwide organization.

Include Local Geography

Usually, you are seeking new members from the local area. So it is important to identify the locations where prospective members are likely to reside or work. These geographical areas should then be included within your set of keywords.

For example, if your club is located within a large metropolitan area, do new members come from all over, or are they most likely to be residents of local communities? If so, include the names of these communities within your keywords.

Does your club meet at a civic facility or in a room provided by a local company or organization? If so, include these as keywords also.

Perhaps your prime club prospects are those who can attend your early morning meeting on their way to work. Identify the local communities and routes they are most likely to drive, and then make these part of your keywords as well. If your club draws members along a major traffic artery, for example, a familiar name (e.g., "I-15 corridor") for that route would be a good keyword.

How to Find the Best Keywords for your Site

Here is a simple way to determine the best keywords to help boost the search engine ranking for your site. Open Google (they own over 75 percent of the search engine market) and type in your primary keywords. Then look at which Websites show up first in the organic search engine returns.

Take a look at every site on the first page of the Google results. Whether they are completely relevant or not to your club's function, these sites are your competitors for your primary keyword(s). To see what keywords their sites are successfully employing to get on the first page of Google results:

1. Click on each site on the first page of the Google returns to open them.

2. Look at the source code for each competitive site. At the top menu of your Internet browser just under the Website address box, there is a function called "View." Click on this to see a drop-down menu. Select "Source" to view the underlying source code for the site.

3. Within the source code (near the top), a block of text usually exists that looks like this example:

```
<META Name="Keywords" Content="public speaking,
Anytown Toastmasters,carleton hills,newport canyon,
communication skills">
```

This is special code that tells the search engines what keywords are considered by the site owner to be most relevant. In this example, this is the Anytown Toastmaster site whose major keywords "public speaking," "anytown toastmasters," and "communication skills," and the site is intended to acquire members from the local communities of Carleton Hills and Newport Canyon.

Make a list of keywords from several relevant searches that score high in the Google results and rank them by priority. They should include:

- Generic words or terms that are most likely to be typed into a search engine box by someone fitting your member profile.

- The primary geographical locations from which membership is most likely to be recruited.

- Your club name

Limit your keyword list to twenty words or phrases. Again, arrange them in order of priority with your most important keywords first.

Because this list is based on appropriate keywords used by competitive Websites that are successfully appearing on the first page of Google returns, you can have confidence that using them for your club site will help to gain similar results.

SAVE THIS LIST OF PRIORITIZED KEYWORDS – IT IS VERY IMPORTANT IN THE NEXT STEPS!

Step 2 – Implement Keyword-Packed Meta Tags for your Club Site

Again, Meta Tags exist in the underlying source code for your club Website. This code can be viewed and edited by using an HTML editor which is provided with ISP tools. GoDaddy's "Website Tonight" solution includes the ability to easily switch back and forth between a

MS Word-like Webpage development tool to the underlying source code.

Within a Website's underlying source code, you are most likely to see HyperTexted Markup Language (HTML) lines of code. Here is an example for our Toastmaster site:

```
<!DOCTYPE HTML PUBLIC "-//W3C//DTD HTML 4.01 Transitional//EN">

<html>

<head>

<title>Anytown Toastmasters –Public Speaking Carleton Hills Newport
Canyon Communication Skills </title>

<Meta Name="Description" Content="Join the Carleton Hills Toastmasters to
begin your journey to confident public speaking and enhanced
communication skills.">

<META Name="Keywords" Content="public speaking,Anytown
Toastmasters,carleton hills,newport canyon,communication skills ">

</head>
```

Notice that the Meta Tags always appear near the top of the source code in-between the <head> and </head> HTML commands.

We are interested in the Title, Description and Keyword Meta Tags. Let's review each to see how you can use them to optimize your club site for search engines.

The Title Tag

The <title> tag contains the title of your club Website that will be displayed in the Internet browser tab, for your Home page (i.e., "index" page) and within search engine returns.

Each page should have a unique title that includes your highest priority keyword(s) for that Webpage. Placing Keywords in the Title tag carries a lot of weight with search engines. Notice how the keywords have been inserted into the Homepage title tag for the previous example of a Toastmaster site.

The Description Meta Tag

The Description Meta Tag contains what a search engine user will see in the abbreviated search engine return for your club site. This should be a sales message that contains your most important keywords.

The Keyword Meta Tag

We just finished discussing how to identify the best keywords for your site. The Keyword Meta Tag tells search engines what the club considers to be the most relevant words or phrases that someone would enter into a search engine box when looking for activities or functions like those offered by the club. The structure of this Tag is:

<Meta Name="Keywords" Content="keyword1,keyword2, ….keywordn">

There is no space after the comma in the keyword list entered under the Content. Alternatively, specific keywords could just be separated by a space:

<Meta Name="Keywords" Content="keyword1 keyword2 …. keywordn">

In this case, keyword phrases can be made up of any combination of the keywords shown within the Content. So, you don't have to repeat keywords that are within specific phrases.

Note that keyword phrases should not include superfluous words like "of" or The." For example, if one of your club's keyword phrases is "garden club of new jersey," it should appear in the keyword Meta Tag Content as "garden club new jersey." And as you can see, keywords are not case sensitive.

It is important to list your keywords in order of importance with the Content segment of the Keyword Meta Tag. Thus, if my keyword priority list were:

Priority	Keyword
1	Public Speaking
2	Anytown Toastmasters
3	Carleton Hills
4	Newport Canyon
5	Communication Skills

Then my Keyword Meta Tag would look like:

<Meta Name="Keywords" Content="public speaking,anytown toastmasters,carelton hills,newport canyon,communication skills"> or alternatively

<Meta Name="Keywords" Content="public speaking anytown toastmasters carelton hills newport canyon communication skills">

Finally, it is best to limit the number of prioritized keywords to twenty or so for optimal results.

Step 3 – Use Keywords within the Page Content

It is very important that you use your primary keywords for each Webpage within the content of that Webpage. This reinforces to search engine crawlers what your club site is about, which helps to ensure that your site is indexed in the fashion you desire.

Sprinkling your primary keywords within a page's textual contents reinforces the importance of those keywords to search engines and visitors alike. When prospective members search keywords on the internet, they are seeking information directly related to the words entered in the search box. Likewise, search engines prosper when their users quickly find relevant Websites.

Primary keywords that relate to the purpose of a page should be included in the first and last paragraph of the page. Others can be injected throughout the page content in a natural fashion. Most experts recommend that keyword density for a Webpage should be in the neighborhood of two-to-six percent. But avoid obvious keyword packing, as search engines will pick this up and ding your site.

It also helps if you have a keyword-packed header (i.e., headline) in the textual content on each page (Header1 in "MS Word talk"). Applying Headers and using bold fonts assists search engine crawlers in determining which textual content is considered most important.

Another way to add keywords to your page content is through the use of "Alt" tags. These insert text that automatically appears whenever you place the mouse cursor over a graphic or photograph. Most Website development tools have the capability to easily insert Alt tags, typically by double clicking on a graphic or photo to bring up a dialog box.

A word of caution - sites that are flash-based with lots of dynamic graphics are ciphers to search engines. To them, it is like trying to read a photograph – they can't! Textual content is the "food" that search engine crawlers crave. Flash-dominated sites have a difficult time ever achieving a high search engine ranking simply because it is hard for crawlers to index them.

Step 4 – Help Search Engine Crawlers by Adding a Robot File to your Site

Often overlooked, adding a small text file or Meta Tag to your Website can make a big difference in search engine ranking. In effect, these features are an invitation to search engine crawlers to index your entire site.

Sometimes you have old Webpages that are no longer used or pages that serve a special purpose, but whose content duplicates those of other pages…a "no no" that will earn your site penalty points. Wouldn't it be nice to have a set of directions to tell search engine crawlers what to look at on your club site while barring entry to other pages?

This is the purpose of a small text file that can be easily created using Microsoft Notepad or a similar tool. The *Robots.txt* file can only be seen by search engines. Here is the format (my comments are in bold):

robots.txt for http://www.myclubsite.com/ **[Anything beginning with a "#" is an optional comment that the crawlers will not read]**

User-agent: * **[Tells search engine crawlers to index the entire site]**

Disallow: /FolderX **[Tells search engine crawlers to skip reading a specific folder ("FolderX" in this example)]**

Disallow: /pagex.html **[Use to prevent crawlers from reading one or more specific Webpages (comma separated)]**

For a typical club Website, the Robots.txt would allow all Webpages and folders to be accessed by search engine crawlers. It would look like this:

robots.txt for http://www.myclubsite.com/

User-agent: *

Disallow:

Having created the file in a text editor like Notepad, save it as a text file into your main Website ("root") directory using the name Robots.txt. The root directory is where all your main Website pages reside (usually the public_html directory).

Alternatively, if you do not wish to exclude any Webpages or folders, a simple Meta Tag can be added to the source code for the index (i.e., Home) page:

<Meta Name="Robots" Content="Index,Follow">

This tells search engine crawlers to index the entire site and follow all links to discover internal pages and externally-linked sites.

Place this Tag anywhere between the <Head> and </Head> commands in the index page source code. Using our earlier example, it would appear like this:

```
<!DOCTYPE HTML PUBLIC "-//W3C//DTD HTML 4.01 Transitional//EN">

<html>

<head>

<title>Anytown Toastmasters – Learn Public Speaking and Communication Skills</title>

<Meta Name="Description" Content="Join the Anytown Toastmasters to begin your journey to confident public speaking and enhanced communication skills.">

<Meta Name="Keywords" Content="public speaking anytown toastmasters carleton hills newport canyon communication skills">

<Meta Name="Robots" Content="Index,Follow">

</head>
```

Step 5 - Include a Site Map designed Specifically for Search Engine Crawlers

An easy way to help search engine crawlers understand the layout and content of your club Website is to add an XML (eXtensible Markup Language) sitemap. It simply lists all the pages in your club Website in a manner that is easily read by search engines. Having an XML sitemap is especially critical to achieving a good Google search engine ranking.

Fortunately, creating an XML sitemap is quick and easy. Just go to www.xml-sitemaps.com and enter your Website address. This site will automatically generate an XML sitemap for you and download it to wherever you wish. Direct it to place the XML sitemap in the root directory of your club Website (normally the public_html directory where the rest of your Webpages reside) where search engine crawlers can easily find it.

Step 6 – Submit your Club Website to the Major Search Engines

It doesn't do any good to create a great club Website if the search engines don't know about it. So after you have completed Steps 1-5, the next step is to directly ask the major search engines to send out their crawlers to index your club's site based on its keywords and XML sitemap.

Simply go to these search engine sites and complete the process to get your site noticed:

Search Engine	Website Submission Address
Google	www.google.com/addurl/
Yahoo	siteexplorer.search.yahoo.com/submit
MSN	search.live.com/docs/submit.aspx
Jayde	submit2.jayde.com

Submitting to these search engines will get the ranking ball rolling for you.

Beware of ads and sites that offer to submit your club website to thousands of search engines for money (or even free). First there are only a handful of meaningful search engines, and submitting to those identified above will ultimately add your site to all of these. Second, most of the Website submission services that populate the Internet are scams that will result in eternal spam coming to your club email contact address.

Submit your Club Site to the Open Project Directory

The Open Project Directory (www.dmoz.org) provides the basis for many search engine *directories*, including Google's. Submission is free and all submissions are reviewed by human editors.

Once you are on the Open Project Directory site, burrow down to the category that best fits your club's nature. Then click on the "Suggest URL" link in the upper right-hand corner to submit your site.

Unfortunately, it takes a long time to get approved by the Open Project Directory, but nonetheless submission is strongly recommended. Meanwhile, you won't be penalized. Direct search engine submission (as previously described) will get your site indexed and on the road to achieving a high search engine ranking.

Search Engine Ranking Takes Time

If your club site is new, expect a considerable delay before it starts showing up in search engine results. This is because the major search engines usually "pigeon hole" new sites for several months to see if they have longevity. So many spam sites are being launched that Google and others now put new sites in a "sand trap" until they demonstrate their legitimacy through continual updates and the establishment of credible external links.

If you follow the guidelines in this book, your new club site should not have any problem showing up in search engine results after a few weeks or months. Meanwhile, you can always direct prospective members to your club URL so that they can review the site.

Step 7 – Add Free Local Listings for your Club Website

Google, Yahoo and MSN all offer geographically-targeted programs that are especially beneficial to gaining local Internet visibility for club Websites. Taking advantage of these free listings is an excellent means of boosting club membership.

Whenever someone located in the zip code where your club address exists searches for your club (or a major keyword associated with your club), your Website will automatically be displayed in a special listing at the top of the first page of the organic search engine results!

Let's take a look at Google first. Just go to their Local Business Center at www.google.com/local/add/login. If you don't have a Google account, you will have to establish one (it's free). After that, simply enter your club information and select a category for its classification. Google will either call you at a phone number you designate or mail you a postcard with a confirmation pin number that must then be entered online to activate your listing.

Once your local Google listing is active, people within your community (i.e., same zip code as the club location) who perform searches using keywords that relate to your category have a good chance of discovering your club. Your free local listing will appear at the top of page one of the Google results, allowing users to quickly get all the information necessary to contact your club (even a map!).

Yahoo offers some good stuff too. They provide a free basic local listing. Go to http://searchmarketing.yahoo.com/local/ll.php and click on "Local Basic Listings" for details.

Likewise, MSN offers a free local listing. To set up yours, go to https://ssl.search.live.com/listings/BusinessSearch.aspx.

But wait – there's more. The Verizon Superpages and Kudzu offer free listings too. Go to https://my.superpages.com/spweb/portals/customer.portal and https://register.kudzu.com/packageSelect.do respectively to sign up.

In summary, these free online local promotions are a bonanza for clubs. They provide local advertising at no cost and also build important search engine links back to your club Website.

Step 8 – Create External Internet Links to your Club Website

Each search engine has a set of unique algorithms it uses to rank your site according to its keywords. A large portion of their formulas is based on a measurement of "popularity." And the most common means of assessing this is by counting the number of incoming links to your club Website from other relevant Websites.

One of the surest ways to increase your Website's search engine ranking is to exchange external links with non-competing complementary sites. All the major search engines award bonus points to sites that have lots of incoming links, registering that as a measure of popularity. Although one-way links from external sites rank higher than two-way links, both contribute to search engine ranking.

There are many pitfalls to avoid in a link exchange program designed to improve your search engine standing. The key is to exchange links only with relevant sites. Otherwise the search engines will ding you. So it's quality, not quantity that counts.

Here are some to tips for places to seek Internet links:

- Local Chamber of Commerce

- If your club is a chapter of a larger organization, be sure to get links to your site published in the district and national Websites.

- Exchange links with similar clubs on a nationwide or global level.

- Look for free Internet directories (commercial and government) that have a category for clubs.

- Participate in blogs that focus on activities offered by your club, being sure to embed a link back to your club site in your comments or biography.

To get bonus points from search engines, use keywords in your external links (called "anchor text"). For example, set up your link to read "Precious Coins," where clicking automatically opens the Website for your coin club.

A word of warning – stay away from "free for all" directories that claim to submit your site to hundreds of other directories. These are usually scams and the search engines will actually penalize your site ranking for doing this because there is no relevancy in the links, many of which relate to porno sites or directories.

With a good link exchange program, you will see your search engine ranking increase over time. Showing up on the first page of Google, Yahoo or MSN when someone enters your site's keywords is better than pay-per-click advertising because it provides credibility. In effect, it's free advertising.

There's another major benefit to having a robust link exchange program. If your site presents a Toastmaster club, for example, and someone is on a site that complements yours in content (say, a site offering public speaking books) and they click on your link, they are doing so because they are truly interested in learning more about your club. This is high-quality traffic directed to your club site without any work on your part!

Chapter 4: Boost Search Engine Ranking by Distributing Free Articles Online

A powerful means of quickly building up one-way external links to your club Website while also bringing interested traffic is to create and distribute free articles over the Internet. Besides investing time and energy, there is no cost associated with this innovative tactic.

Free Articles – What are They?

A free article is one prepared by someone in your club dealing with a relevant topic. It is not a written advertisement for your club, but rather addresses a germane subject of interest to others.

For example, if you belong to a sewing club, prepare an article on the merits of different threads or discuss patterns. Likewise, a rifle club could prepare an article discussing gun safety or new hunting regulations. A Toastmaster club can present an article on speaking styles, how to handle hecklers when addressing large audiences, or the importance of vocal variety.

The parameters for distributing a free article online are generally:

- Use Microsoft Word or similar tool to prepare the article.

- The article must contain information of value to a targeted audience.

- The optimal length should be 300 to 1,000 words.

- It should be structured with a title (and optional subtitle) and paragraph breaks.

- There should normally be no more than two active hyperlinks in the article.

- Prepare a short article abstract as well.

- Include an author biography with an embedded hyperlink back to your club's Website.

How are Free Articles Distributed?

There are several Websites on the Internet that are devoted to distribution of free articles and content for use by other sites, blogs and newsletters. There is no cost to establishing a free account with these distribution sites. Each has its own rules, but they are all generally compatible in their guidelines.

Setting up initial accounts takes a little time, but you only have to go through that process once. Thereafter, your club can submit as many articles as it likes. Recommended article distribution sites for you to evaluate are:

Website	Address
EzineArticles	www.ezinearticles.com
GoArticles	www.goarticles.com
ArticlesFactory	www.articlesfactory.com
ArticlesBase	www.articlebase.com
GiveMeArticles	www.givemearticles.com

What is the Benefit for My Club?

Distributing free articles is the super highway to building one-way external links to your club Website from other relevant sites worldwide.

These articles are picked up as content fillers by Websites, blogs and email newsletters around the world. And one requirement for using them is to retain the author's biography, which (as you recall) contains an active hyperlink back to your club Website.

So when your article becomes embedded within the content of another Website, blog or newsletter, the active link goes along with it. And these entities typically do not delete this content at a future date; rather, they archive this material online, so your link still gives your site positive points with search engines as a measure of popularity.

Let's say your club writes one article and places on each of the five free distribution sites previously referenced. Suppose the article gets picked up by 25 Websites, blogs or newsletters at each location. That is a total of 125 external links from relevant online sources that have just been generated for our club Website!

And many of the sites consuming your article already have high search engine ranking, so when someone searches for subject matter related to the article content, your summary may come up on the first page as part of another Website. That means your embedded club link gains high Internet visibility as well.

If your club simply contributes a short article every month to these free distribution sites, imagine how many external incoming links could be generated! This is one of the fastest – and certainly cheapest – ways to quickly build up your club's Website ranking with all the major search engines.

Chapter 5: Use Targeted Google Pay-Per-Click Advertising to Gain Instant Internet Visibility

If your keywords have a lot of competition, it can take a long time to gain visibility on the Internet for your site even after optimizing it for the search engines. And for a new site, you have to wait out the "sand trap" effect, which can be several months or more.

Bottom line – it could take awhile before your club Website starts showing up in search engine results and even longer before the site makes it into the first three pages of results. Existing sites that are overhauled for search engine optimization typically have a shorter journey, but can still expect some time to pass depending on the competition for club keywords and how focused the site is on recruiting members from specific locations.

In the meantime, there is an inexpensive way to immediately show up on page one of search engine results by using very targeted Google Pay-Per-Click (PPC) advertising.

What is PPC Advertising?

When you bring up Google in your Internet browser, you will notice a vertical column of ads along the right-hand side.

For example, if I am hunting for a sewing club and enter the keyword "sewing" into the Google search box, I get a large number of organic search engine results, plus a number of PPC ads related to "sewing." See figure 1 on the next page.

PPC advertising is a unique approach that emerged with the dawn of the Internet. The underlying concept is simple. PPC ads only appear when someone enters a keyword in the search box related to the ad, and advertisers are only charged when that same person actually clicks on their ad.

Figure 1. Google PPC Advertising Example

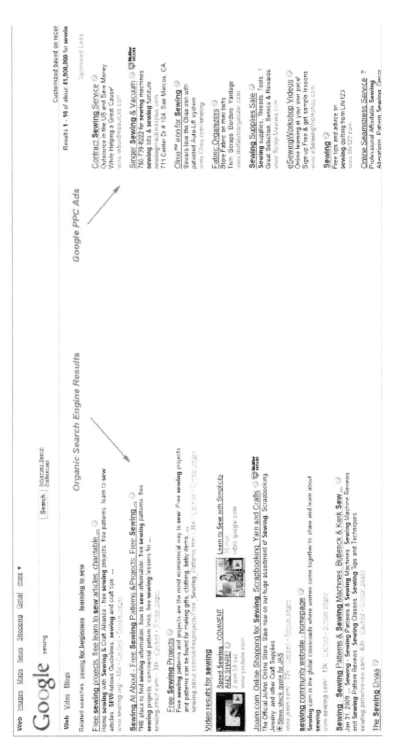

Chapter 5: Boost Internet Visibility with PPC Advertising

Why Google?

 Google "owns" roughly 75 percent of the search engine marketplace. Most people do Internet searches using Google. Hence, it only makes sense to focus your scarce advertising budget on the search engine where you get the "most bang for the buck."

Yahoo and MSN offer similar PPC advertising programs, but the viewing audience is much smaller. If yours is a local non-profit club, then your advertising budget is small and must be targeted for maximum results.

Is Learning Google PPC Advertising Hard?

Setting up and using Google PPC advertising can be a complex undertaking. However, I am going to share some parameter settings later in this Chapter that will make it much easier to accomplish and prevent your club from accidentally being charged a bundle for useless advertising.

Learning the basics of Google PPC advertising is not hard, but it does require dedicated time. Explaining how everything works in Google "AdWords," which is what they call their PPC advertising program, is beyond the scope of this book. Fortunately, Google offers good tutorials, and I strongly recommend that you go visit their learning center at www.google.com/adwords/learningcenter/ before embarking on a club advertising campaign. There you will find several easy-to-understand video tutorials that cover the basics of PPC advertising. If you enter "google adwords tutorial" into the Google search engine, you will also find many independent tutorials to investigate.

Learning the basics is not hard. But understanding how to best set a multitude of parameters for a club advertising campaign is where skill and experience comes into play. Doing this correctly will yield an effective advertising campaign with minimal cost.

The Mechanics of Using Google PPC Advertising

Let's start by giving an overview of the mechanics that govern Google PPC advertising. There are several aspects that interplay to determine the effectiveness of an advertising campaign:

- The keywords you select for your club advertising campaign should include those around which your optimized Website is built. Google provides free tools for performing keyword research if you wish to add others.

- Keyword bids are established using Google-provided tools. Here, you are competing against other advertisers to have your club ad appear whenever someone enters one of your keywords in the Google search engine box. The amount you bid for a keyword helps to determine the vertical positioning of your ad in response to a search within Google. The higher your bid, the higher your ad position, and the more likely it is that your ad will appear on the first page of Google search results.

- Google allows you to set a daily budget for your club advertising campaign. This is the maximum amount that your club is willing to spend each day. Google will spread your ads evenly throughout the day in a fashion they expect to maximize your daily coverage within budget constraints. The larger your daily budget, the higher the frequency of your ad appearances.

- Your account is only charged when someone actually clicks on your PPC ad. Thus, your ad could appear one thousand times per day, but only receive five clicks. Your club is only charged for the five ad clicks, and the amount charged is the prevailing rate per click as determined by Google, which is often less than the amount you bid for the keyword.

- When a Google user clicks on one of your club ads, they are automatically taken to one of the following based on parameters you designate in the advertising set-up process: 1) your club Website Home page, 2) a specific page in your club Website, or 3) a special "landing page" where your sole purpose is to convince someone to contact your club about membership.

- If a landing page is employed as the destination for ad "click-throughs," Google includes a mechanism to report the return on investment (ROI) for your advertising campaign, assuming that your club's measurement of success is the number of people contacting you as a result of the PPC advertising campaign. That is, how many leads did my club get, and how much are we paying for each lead. This allows you to gauge the effectiveness of your PPC advertising.

How Can PPC Advertising Benefit my Club?

PPC advertising offers several benefits for clubs:

- It provides instant visibility for your club Website while you are waiting to escape from the Google "sand trap" and during the time it takes for your optimized site to bubble up in search engine rankings.

- Done right, Google PPC advertising will place your ad on the first page of search engine returns where it is highly visible whenever someone searches the Internet using one of your keywords.

- Since the ad only appears when someone enters one or more of the keywords designated in your advertising campaign, your ad is visible to the user at the exact moment they are searching for the functions and activities provided by your club.

- Your club is only charged for the ad whenever someone actually clicks on it. Otherwise, it is free advertising!

The Secrets of Setting Up Inexpensive PPC Advertising to Promote Club Membership

Now that you understand the basics of Google AdWords PPC advertising, it is time to set up your own club campaign. In this section, you learn how to set critical parameters to get maximum results from your AdWords advertising within a limited budget.

Remember, although Google offers a first-timer starter edition to help new users get through the process of setting up a campaign, Google's objective is to get as much money as possible from advertisers. My objective is to help your club get the best results without spending a bundle!

Set Up a Google AdWords Account

Begin by going to www.google.com and clicking on "Advertising Programs." This will take you to a starting point for implementing your PPC advertising. Click on "Get Started with AdWords" to begin.

You will need a credit or debit card to set up a Google AdWords account. And if you don't already have a free Google account, you will be asked to establish one as part of the PPC set-up process.

Begin by selecting the "Standard Edition" solution. Otherwise, you will not be able to use many of the cost control and targeting parameters I am going to demonstrate.

Recommended Campaign Settings

Google will lead you through the process of setting of a new AdWords account. Step-by-step, you will be asked to choose certain parameters. Don't worry about making a mistake at this point – you can always change your settings once a PPC account is established simply by clicking on "Edit Campaign Settings."

Here are considerations and recommendations for setting up your PPC advertising campaign:

- Under Budget Options, initially set your daily budget low. For example, a local non-profit club should look at a daily budget of $2 to $3. You can always change this figure later based on campaign performance statistics.

Remember, this is not the amount your club will actually be charged everyday. Rather, it is the maximum amount, since a charge is applied only when someone actually clicks on one of your club ads.

If you should consume your club's daily budget, the ads will stop running for that day. However, this rarely happens in the case of local clubs.

One way to determine whether your daily budget is too low is to enter your primary keyword in Google and then see if your ad appears among all the ads (i.e., look through all the Google search pages to view all ads). If not, consider increasing the daily budget to boost the display frequency of your ad campaign.

- Under <u>Networks and Bidding</u>, only select Google Search and Network Partners (includes AOL, etc.). Do not choose "The Content Network" as this allows your ads to also be displayed on individual Websites. Without much more expertise than you need to learn, this will result in a frivolous waste of money.

  Also, select only "Desktop and Laptop Computers" under "Device Platform." This will prevent your ads from running on iPods and mobile phones, where the likelihood of generating good membership leads is much less.

- Under <u>Scheduling and Serving</u>, select "Run at select times only." There is no sense in using up your budget to run club ads at midnight, so set up the run times for each day of the week covering the period that prospective members are likely to be online. I have had good luck with running ads from 5 AM until 10 PM on week days and 5 AM until Midnight on weekends.

  For "Ad Serving," it is best to initially set the ads to rotate evenly until you gain some feedback to see which ones are generating the most click-throughs. After a few weeks, set this parameter to focus on serving the best-performing ads.

- Under <u>Target Audience</u> is where your campaign can become really focused. First, select one or more languages (affects the language version of Google in which your ads will appear). Usually, this is "English."

  Now, a major success key for membership recruitment and keeping your costs low is to get very specific on the geographical locations where your ads will be visible. Remember the location keywords used in optimizing your Website? You probably want to use the same ones here.

  Ask yourself, where am I likely to find new club members? How far away from our club address are prospective members likely to reside? Then click on "Edit" under "Locations" to set specific parameters. Under the *custom* tab in the resultant dialogue box that appears, you can set a radius in miles around your club address where your ads will be seen. This means that only desktop or laptop users located within "x" miles of your club's physical address, for example, will see your ads when they enter relevant keywords into the search box. And you have the option of excluding certain areas or creating specific target areas.

  This is powerful stuff – be sure to use it to get maximum exposure of your ads to the right audience!

Generally speaking, be conservative in your initial campaign settings and remember that you can always adjust them later on. But wait until you gain some history with the campaign. Then take "baby steps." Make a little change, give it a week or so to see what impact it has, and then tweak your campaign again if necessary.

Choose your PPC Keywords

The appearance of your ads is triggered by the entry of specifics words or phrases in the Google search box. Hence, proper keyword selection is a very important part of a PPC advertising campaign.

Google offers a number of free tools to assist with keyword selection (including identifying synonyms), showing bid competition and expected traffic. For most local clubs focused on leveraging the Internet to solely building membership, these tools are not germane. In fact, it is easy to find so many keywords that the effectiveness of your ad campaign can become diluted.

Certainly, you want to include the keywords on which the club Website is optimized. This should include your club name, the names of local communities from which new members are likely to come, and words or phrases indicative of the major benefits or activities that your club offers.

For clubs seeking new members, it is a good idea to construct keyword phrases that combine the club name or function with a location. Using the previous Toastmaster example, likely keywords phrases would be:

toastmasters carleton hills

toastmasters newport canyon

public speaking carleton hills

public speaking newport canyon

This is especially true if your club is a local chapter of a national organization and has competitive chapters located in adjacent areas from which you are trying to recruit new members.

Likewise, if your club is a local chapter trying to recruit new members within a metropolitan area with lots of competitive chapters, your Website may have a tough time coming up on page one of Google when someone is hunting for a club by searching on its broad name. For example, someone searching for "Toastmasters" in San Diego would receive dozens of organic returns. But the Rancho Bernardo Toastmasters ran a low-cost PPC ad with one of its keywords being "toastmasters." So whenever someone within San Diego searches for a toastmaster club, the Rancho Bernardo Toastmasters ad comes up on page one even though its Website may not come up until much later in the organic search engine returns!

Start out with your core keywords and maybe add one or two that Google recommends. But avoid trying to compete with highly popular keywords, as this will drive up your costs. A club ad campaign can get as much mileage by focusing on keywords and phrases that are "second tier" rather than consuming its budget of the most popular ones. And never forget that Google wants you to spend as much as possible.

There are four ways to match entries in the Google search engine box to PPC keywords:

Match Type	Definition
Broad Match	Allows your ad to show on similar phrases and relevant variations. This is a loose match that generates more ad appearances. **Recommended as a starting point for most clubs**, as it allows you to experiment to see which keywords get the most ad appearances ("impressions") and perform the best for the money spent.
"Phrase Match"	Enclose keyword or phrase in quotation marks. Ads only appear when the search engine entry includes an exact match of the phrase in the same order. Good way to control costs and get better matches.

Match Type	Definition
[Exact Match]	The most targeted option. Enclose a keyword or phrase in bracket marks. Allows your ad to show only for searches that match the exact phrase exclusively in the same order without any other terms. Results in fewer ad appearances, but usually more clicks when a match occurs.
Negative Match	Place a negative sign in front of the keyword. Ensures your ad doesn't show for any search that includes that term. These can co-exist with your positive keywords. Use as necessary to optimize your campaign.

Placing your Keyword Bids

Google has some powerful tools that estimate the number of click-throughs your ads may receive for specific keywords. Take these with a grain of salt, considering that your club's PPC advertising is probably focused on a small geographical area.

It is likely that there will be little competition for keywords that are a combination of your club name and geographical location. A good way to determine what competition your keywords (words by themselves and in specific phrases) have is to enter each in the Google search box and then see what pops up in the advertising column. If nothing pops up, you are home free. You have no competition. In this case, simply place the minimum bid required by Google, which may be just a few cents!

*Here is a secret Google would prefer you didn't know about –
there is little or no PPC advertising being performed for non-profit
clubs, so there is usually no competition for keyword bidding that
includes a club name. In other words, PPC advertising using club-
oriented keywords is dirt cheap!*

If you feel it is necessary to bid against strongly competitive
keywords, such as bidding for "public speaking" when you are
marketing a Toastmaster club, then do so cautiously. Never try to
outbid the leaders. Rather, settle for a "middle of the road" bid and
emphasize your competitive differentiation PPC ad (such as a much
lower cost than a commercial solution to improve public speaking
skills). As long as your ad shows up within the first three pages of
Google results, its stark contrast will get results.

Constructing PPC Ads

Google PPC ads allow only a limited space for text, so you need
to make the words count. All ads have a similar format:

Headline
Text talking about benefits
Text talking about benefits
Your club URL

Here are some tips that will help your ad(s) get the best results:

- Remember that your club ad is an advertisement whose purpose is to "sell" prospective members on the benefits of joining your club. Treat it so.

- Place your club name in the headline if it is a keyword that someone is likely to enter into the Google search box. Otherwise, focus your headline on a key benefit for which a Google search is likely to be performed.

- If you are targeting certain geographical locations, make sure the location is included in the ad headline or text. Having critical keywords in the headline gives your ad more relevance to Google, and it will be displayed more often and in a better position than are ads which lack one or more of the keywords entered into the Google search box.

- Use the text portion to succinctly sell the benefits of your club. Offer special incentives, if any. Capitalize each word in the text. Use abbreviations only if they are readily understandable.

- Capitalize the first letter of words within your club domain name (URL) if it consists of multiple words.

Here are examples of ads employing these practices:

Sewing Club Petersville
Learn Sewing Techniques. Free
Patterns and Material Discounts.
www.PetersvilleSewingClub.com

Oil Painting Club SmallTown
Free Mentoring for Beginners
& Experienced. Only $15/Mo.
www.SmallTownPainters.com

Public Speaking Training
Learn Communication/Speaking Skills
$45 – Rancho Bernardo Toastmasters
www.RBToastmasters.com

How to Invest & Make Money
Join our Club; Learn How to Pick
Stock Mkt & Mutual Fund
Winners!
www.RoseMillInvestors.com

Another thing to keep in mind during ad construction is that your goal is to entice likely new members while minimizing advertising costs. Hence, be sure your ad is not misleading or open to misinterpretation. Otherwise, you will receive superfluous click-throughs that drive up costs. For example, if you only want to attract prospective members from a local community, be sure to include the name of the community in your ad. Likewise, if your club is for seniors, it would be wise to mention that ("55+"). If you have special membership requirements, include that as well (e.g., "Licensed Pilots…"). The more targeted your ad, the better the results and the lower the costs.

PPC Advertising Requires Monitoring

PPC advertising is not something you set up and then walk away from. It requires constant monitoring and tweaking, especially at the beginning.

Google AdWords includes a variety of useful online reports to help you track and analyze PPC results and expenses. Learn to use these, for they are key to achieving the best results within budgetary limitations.

Frequent AdWords tweaking is necessary. Keyword bids may need adjusting to retain optimal ad positioning. Your daily budget might require boosting if your club's ads are not appearing with the desired frequency, or you may find that your ads are receiving more clicks than you anticipated and the daily budget needs to be reduced to curtail expenses.

When your PPC advertising is initially launched, expect to review results at least twice weekly. Once the campaign is adjusted based on actual results, it will find a "sweet spot" where ad positioning and the number of impressions satisfies your goals. This normally takes several weeks. Thereafter, you can monitor results on a bi-weekly basis.

What Results can I Expect?

Expected results from PPC advertising are dependent upon several factors:

- How your PPC advertising campaign parameters are defined.

- How well known your organization is (e.g., a Toastmaster club versus a new local gardening club).

- The effectiveness of your club Website and/or landing page.

- How competitive your club keywords are.

Generally speaking, PPC advertising campaigns receive a click-through rate of one-half-to-five percent. Thus, your club ad may appear a thousand times per month, but only a small number of Google users will actually click on it. And this is good. You only want those who are truly interested to click on your ad(s). This keeps your advertising costs down while hopefully generating high quality membership leads.

Of those clicking on your club ad, expect 3-to-10 percent to contact the club about membership. This figure can be much higher if your PPC ads take "clickers" to a special landing page (see the next chapter).

Even if your club receives no direct leads from its PPC advertising, it still gains Internet visibility while your Website is bubbling up in search engine rankings. And many people will simply enter the URL in your ad into their browser to go directly to your club Website. This free advertising costs nothing because Google only charges the club when someone actually clicks on the ad!

Chapter 6: Improve PPC Advertising Results with a Landing Page

You may also discover that although your ads receive click-throughs, your club is not receiving many inquiries from prospective members.

This could be a consequence of the PPC ad taking them to your Website Home page where they get lost or lose their attention span. At minimum, a PPC ad should take those who click on it to a relevant page in your club Website that quickly grabs their attention and makes the ad clicker want to explore your site further. I suggest the "About Our Club" page, or a page with lots of photos that provides an overview of the club and its membership benefits.

One way to improve PPC advertising results is to have the ad automatically take clickers to a special "landing page." This is a standalone page in your Club Website that can only be reached by clicking on a PPC ad. Its sole purpose is to entice prospective members to contact your club. In addition to phone or email contact information, it is recommended that a "lead capture" form be included. Submitted form information can be automatically emailed to a designated person in your club for fast phone or email follow-up with the prospective member.

Using a landing page in conjunction with PPC advertising can dramatically improve results. It is not unusual to see up to 25 percent deciding to contact the club for more information.

Hosting vendors (ISPs) typically provide a means for form creation that 1) allows you to specify an email address to where the form results are sent, and 2) to designate which page in your Website the visitor is automatically taken to after submitting the form. GoDaddy with its "WebSite Tonight" tool makes this easy to set up.

After submitting the completed form, an interested visitor should be automatically taken to a "thank you" Webpage where your standard Website links allow him/her to further explore what the club has to offer.

There are several advantages to using one or more landing pages in conjunction with PPC advertising:

- An uncluttered, persuasive sales argument can be presented on the landing page, with the objective of convincing the reader that your club offers the benefits which they are seeking.

- Only those with a true interest in the club are likely to contact your club, so the quality of landing page "leads" is high.

- Using a landing page allows your club to set up an ROI calculation within Google AdWords. If your club were a business, then contacts from your landing page would be sales leads. The whole purpose of doing PPC advertising would be to generate these sales leads.

  If your landing page funnels ad clickers through a sales presentation to a contact form, then any visitor who arrives at the subsequent "thank you" page represents a sales lead, and this provides a basis for computing the "return on investment" (ROI) for your advertising campaign.

For example, if your club spends $12 monthly for PPC advertising and receives three emailed forms, the average cost per new member lead is only four dollars.

Google AdWords includes tools that can automatically be notified when a click-through visitor arrives at your club's "thank you" page. This will be reflected in their online reports as a sales lead generated as a consequence of PPC advertising and the average "cost per lead" will be automatically calculated for you.

If you include an email address or phone number on your landing page, be sure to include any results from these contact channels in computing the average cost per lead.

Chapter 7: Recruit New Members through Online Social Media

The Internet has recently evolved with the introduction of interactive social media. These use Internet and mobile-based technologies to facilitate the exchange of information among people. They allow people to exchange text messages, share photos and upload audio and video recordings.

Social media is a fun way of keeping in touch with relatives, friends and groups. And these innovative forums have captured the attention of Internet users of all ages. Social media has caught on like a fast-moving wildfire.

Because social media allows the creation of Webpages and "groups" with similar interests, this medium can be used for marketing purposes. In fact, social media is a free vehicle for promoting your club (and its Website address) among local, national and worldwide audiences, many of whom may be potential club members.

The major downside of social media is that you have to keep on top of it. Due to its interactive nature, reviewing and responding to a slew of daily messages and comments is necessary for social media to be an effective club marketing vehicle. Your club may want to appoint specific members to be responsible for maintaining these daily communications.

Here, we will look at some of the most popular social media sites and discuss how to utilize them for online club promotion.

Facebook

Facebook (www.facebook.com) is one of the better known and biggest social media sites. Founded in 2004, it already has over 70 million members! Joining is free. Facebook is probably the best social media choice for most clubs to promote themselves online for the purpose of gaining Internet visibility and recruiting new members.

Setting up a Facebook Webpage for your club is free and easy to do. Just select "Club" during the initial *Create a Facebook Page* process. Doing this presents an opportunity to promote your club to all (or targeted) Facebook members and to exchange messages with those who express interest in becoming club members.

Be sure to place club information in your *Profile* page. Optionally join a *Network* for a local area where prospective members live. Under *Settings*, you can also click *Groups* and then create your own club Group (only group members can exchange messages). If you wish, advertise club meeting schedules in *Upcoming Events*. You can also create a *Friends* list for distributing and exchanging information with your club members.

For quick answers to questions, click on the *Help* link at the bottom of the Facebook page. It offers a search function and a *Getting Started* guide.

YouTube

YouTube (www.YouTube.com) is a free online video streaming service that allows anyone to view and share videos that have been uploaded by its members.

You can create your own YouTube channel for your club. This affords an opportunity to create a profile for your club with a link back to your website URL.

Create a "Guru" account and upload videos whose content relates to club activities. If you have a sewing club, your videos could explain how to perform certain stitches or work with different type of materials and pattern designs. A Toastmaster club could record and upload videos addressing different aspects of public speaking. You get the idea.

So, if you have someone in your club who is good at making videos, YouTube might be an opportunity to build up a large club following among worldwide prospective members. Word spreads, and news of your informative videos should trickle down to possible local club members as well.

MySpace

MySpace (www.MySpace.com) is a personal online network where you can create a private community for your club. You can then view connections between members and their friends, inviting new contacts to join the community.

MySpace works best for clubs that target younger members (teens and twenties). Look under *Groups* to see what's hot at the moment. Generally speaking, MySpace is not a good choice for clubs focused on attracting adult members.

Twitter

Twitter (www.Twitter.com) is a relatively new social media. As prefaced on their site, "Twitter is a service for friends, family, and co–workers to communicate and stay connected through the exchange of quick, frequent answers to one simple question: What are you doing?"

Twitter offers marketing opportunities for clubs because a club page can be established and then you can troll Twitter for prospective new members.

The best approach is to identify individuals or organizations whose profile complements your club membership criteria, then reviewing their "followers" and electing to "follow" those who seem to have potential. Many of those who you choose to "follow" will also select you (your club) to "follow" in return.

Over time, you can assemble a strong following of prospective members. Since these people are exposed to your Twitter profile which talks about your club and gives a Website link, some may elect to visit your club site and join up.

If you do Twitter, be prepared to spend a couple of hours daily responding to messages in order to keep your followers active.

Start a Club Blog

One way to keep your Website fresh and create a following is to start a club blog. GoDaddy (www.GoDaddy.com) offers this option when hosting a Website. Blogger (www.Blogger.com), a blog tool offered by Google, and WordPress (www.WordPress.com) are two popular free sites for setting up blogs. All include templates and easy-to-use tools for creating and maintaining a blog.

A club blog allows members to post short articles and comments on a variety of activities related to club activities and functions. Someone in the club should have the authority to review all posts before they go live. This person can also decide whether public comments to blog entries should go live or be deleted.

Every time a blog is updated, your club can let the world know about it by using Ping-O-Matic (www.pingomatic.com) to automatically notify blog update distribution sites and search engines.

Just be sure to promote the blog on your club Website and include an active link which opens it in a new browser window. If short blog articles are published on a regular basis, the blog will gather a following of interested people, some of which may become new club members. By including your club Website link in freely distributed (using Ping-O-Matic) blog entries, your club can build up links on other sites. Thus a blog can become both a powerful club recruitment tool for new members and a means to build search engine ranking.

Chapter 8: Other Online Recruitment Tactics

Once your club has a Website platform for Internet marketing and perhaps Google PPC advertising running, there are several low or no-cost activities to promote yourselves within the local community. These will be discussed here.

Submit Press Releases to Local Community Websites

Press releases are like free advertising. And they are one of the best ways to promote your club within a local community.

All that is required is to prepare a one-to-two page press release about a newsworthy activity or event regarding your club. For example, perhaps it has received an award, or maybe you are planning an event of interest to the community. Or you could just write a release about how the club serves the community.

Press releases require a certain format. You can easily learn how to prepare a press release by visiting sites like www.PRWeb.com or www.PublicityInsider.com. Remember to include an embedded link to your club Website in the content or press release contact information.

Once your release is prepared, research local online community and news Websites. Check out the local Chamber of Commerce site. Then either call them or email them your press release. Include photos with captions if you have them.

Besides online forums, send club press releases to local newspapers and periodicals as well. They may print them as content fillers or as a community service.

Advertise Free in Craigslist

Craigslist.org provides free advertising by metropolitan areas. Open an account and place your club ad under Community Activities. Be sure to include contact information. The only downside to Craigslist is that ads must be renewed every week or so.

Start a Club Email Newsletter

Email newsletters cost nothing and contribute immensely to building club membership. They are easy to prepare and often get forwarded to friends and relatives who might be prospective club members. Newsletters are also a great way to nurture existing membership through monthly updates.

Your club can send either text-based newsletters by using Microsoft Outlook and setting up a Contact group, or you can invest in graphical templates for more colorful newsletters. Either approach is effective.

The important thing is to distribute a club newsletter with regularity. The newsletter does not have to be long. It can contain interesting club stories, announcement of (or reminders for) upcoming club events, awards, jokes, anecdotes, or whatever. The newsletter can present an entire article, or else provide the first paragraph with a link to the full article on the club Website. Again, be sure to include club contact information and an active link to your website in the email newsletter. By sending out the newsletter on a monthly basis, membership retention will increase and recruitment of new members through viral marketing will occur as it gets passed around.

Also recruit new members by placing a newsletter subscription box on your club Website. Ask only for a first name and email address. Clicking on the submit button should take the new subscriber to either a "thank you" page or the most current edition of your club newsletter.

Archive past editions of club newsletters on your Website, accessible by a master index page. You will be surprised how many

Website visitors like to assess the merits of joining a club by reading their old newsletters.

It is important to comply with CAN-SPAM laws when distributing an email newsletter. Otherwise, your club could be labeled as a "spammer," and the club Website could become blacklisted. You do not want this to happen. Just keep two things in mind: 1) never send unsolicited email. Stick to club members and those who have requested the newsletter, and 2) Always provide a means to unsubscribe from the newsletter, such as email address or link to a Website page where the unsubscribe procedure is quick and easy. A club address is also mandatory.

List management is important too. Effective attention to new subscribers and those who wish to unsubscribe is a critical factor in successful email newsletter management.

If your subscriber list gets large and list management becomes burdensome, evaluate upgrading to an Internet-based email newsletter service. Some are free, while others start out with a low monthly fee based on the number of subscribers. Most offer a free trial period. One that I suggest is www.ConstantContact.com. Enter "email newsletter" in Google to discover a host of others.

Promote your Website Address Offline Too

One method of promoting your club is to have club business cards prepared with your contact information, including a phone number, email address and the club Website URL. These can be handed out to acquaintances, placed on bulletin boards in stores and business lunch rooms, college campuses, etc.

Likewise, prepare inexpensive flyers and distribute them around the local community from which you wish to recruit members. Again, these should include complete contact information.

Conclusion

Hopefully by now you realize the magnitude of free or low-cost promotion your club can achieve online. You have learned about a variety of techniques to attract new club members using the Internet. And you feel this is something that, with a little work, you and your fellow members can accomplish. You don't have to be a rocket scientist to put the Internet to work for your club.

Your club can use any or all of the online strategies presented within these pages. Mix and match to suit your skill levels, time constraints, budget and membership profiles. Experiment and use what works best. None of the activities presented here is going to break your piggy bank.

The only critical requirement for successful online marketing is to have an independent, optimized Website. In the online environment, this is the "sun" around which all club recruitment activities orbit. It is your virtual clubhouse. Without a Website, your club must resort to expensive offline advertising and manual networking to recruit new members.

A well-done Website also lends credibility to a club and makes it attractive to prospective members. It is a 24/7 neon sign selling the benefits of membership to those who are already searching for what your club has to offer.

To be successful, you and your fellow club members only have to commit time and energy to launch your own online marketing strategy. It may require some work on your part to optimize your club Website for search engines, or to learn how to leverage simple Google PPC advertising tactics. However, this is a small price to pay if you want to see your club membership dramatically expand over the next year.

The effort is worth it. These methods have been tested. THEY WORK! If you put energy into promoting your club online and capturing "sales leads" in the fashion explained in these pages, you will succeed. Within a few months, your club will see positive results. Ultimately, your only problem may be whether you need a larger meeting facility. Good luck, and enjoy the journey!

About the Author

Al Kernek has thirty years of hands-on marketing experience in both Fortune 500 firms and entrepreneurial start-up companies. He has an extensive background in Internet marketing and business consulting.

His credentials include a master's degree in business management, numerous courses in high-tech marketing, plus many industry and company awards for outstanding achievement.

Al has also published two previous books which are widely available in retail and online outlets:

- One for real estate agents interested in email newsletters. This can be found at http://www.RENewsletter.com, a Website dedicated to providing Internet marketing tools and services for Realtors.

- Another for small business people and entrepreneurs seeking to market their business online. See www.SmallBizSmartMarketing.com for details.

As a member of the Rancho Bernardo Toastmasters (www.RBToastmasters.com), Al personally derived and tested the online marketing strategies shared in this book. They proved hugely successful for his club, and they can work for your club too.

Among Al's many interests are a passion for bike riding along the California coastline, skiing, good mystery and horror novels, charitable works and mentoring small businesses. He resides with his wife and an assortment of critters in San Diego, California.

Please contact Al with any questions or comments at his business email: akernek@smallbizsmartmarketing.com. All comments are welcomed.

www.ingramcontent.com/pod-product-compliance
Lightning Source LLC
Chambersburg PA
CBHW051114050326
40690CB00006B/787